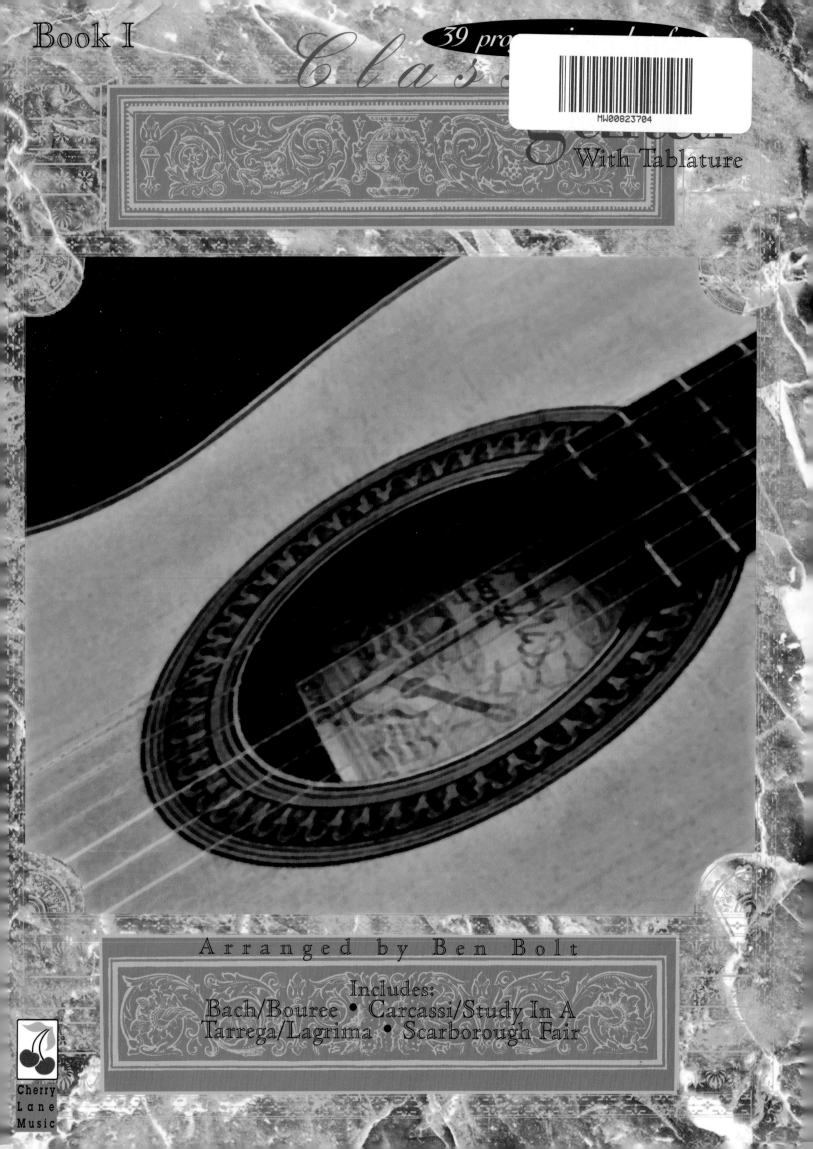

Book I

39 pro...

Clas...

...guitar

With Tablature

Arranged by Ben Bolt

Includes:
Bach/Bouree • Carcassi/Study In A
Tarrega/Lagrima • Scarborough Fair

Cherry Lane Music

39 progressive solos for

Classical
guitar
With Tablature

Book I

Arranged by Ben Bolt

Contents Book I

Contents Book II

Each book is available with CD or with cassette. Numbers in boxes refer to CD and cassette tracks.

1 *

STUDY 1

Arr. Ben Bolt

Dionisio Aguado

* Numbers in boxes refer to CD and cassette tracks.

STUDY 2

Arr. Ben Bolt

Matteo Carcassi

Prelude

STUDY 3

Arr. Ben Bolt

Matteo Carcassi

Andante

* Track 2 contains Study 2 and Study 3.

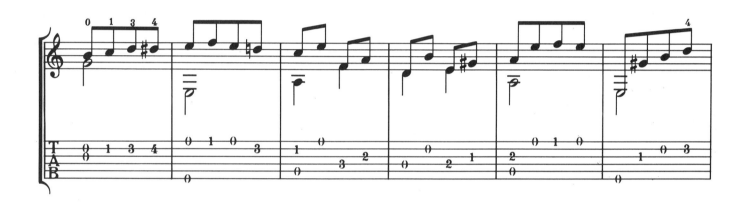

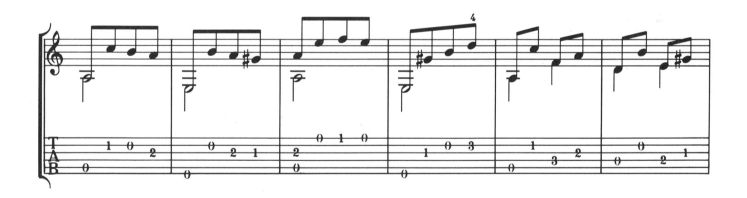

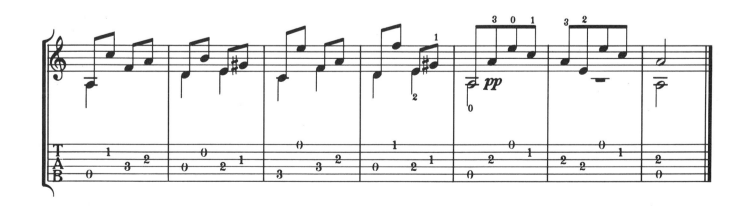

3 *

STUDY 4

Arr. Ben Bolt

Matteo Carcassi

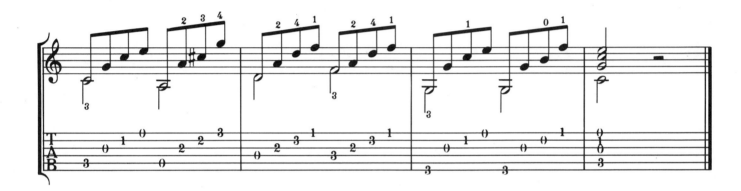

STUDY 5

Arr. Ben Bolt

Matteo Carcassi

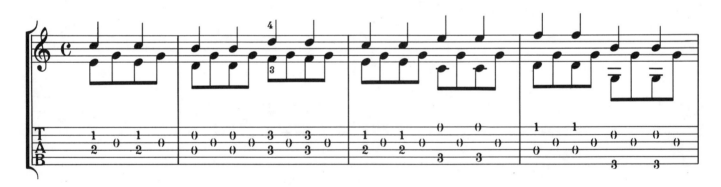

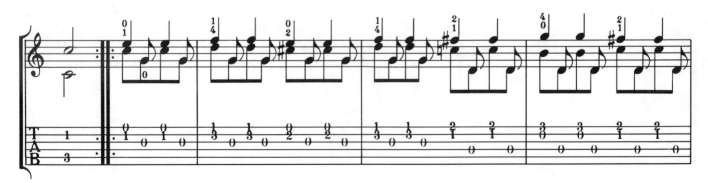

* Track 3 contains Study 4 and Study 5.

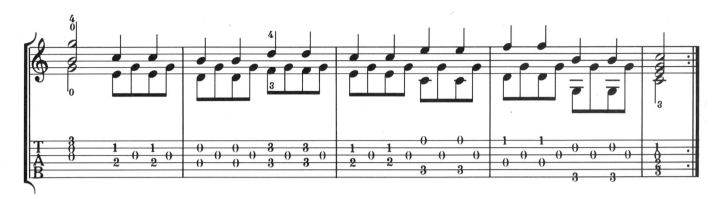

4

STUDY 6

Arr. Ben Bolt

Mauro Giuliani

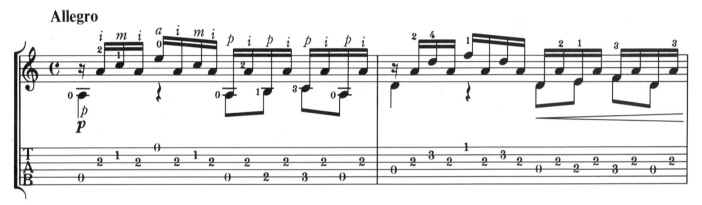

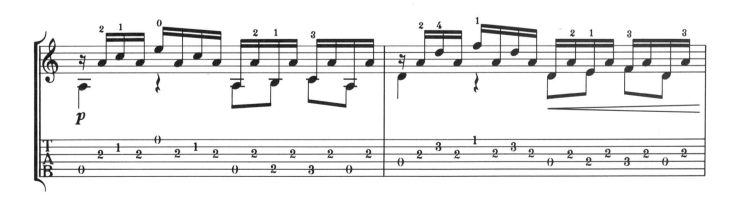

7

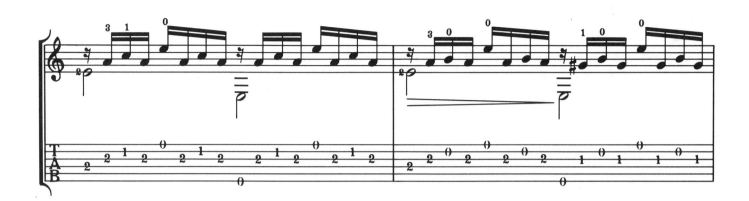

5

STUDY 7

Arr. Ben Bolt

Matteo Carcassi

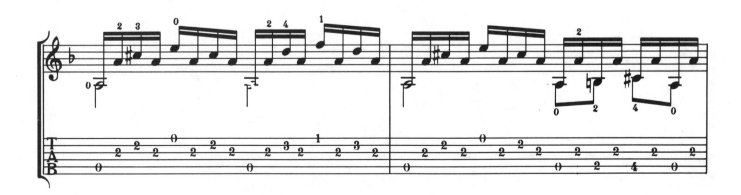

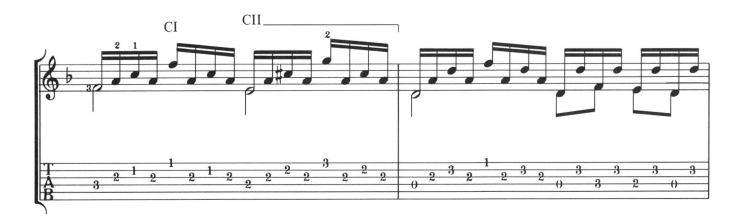

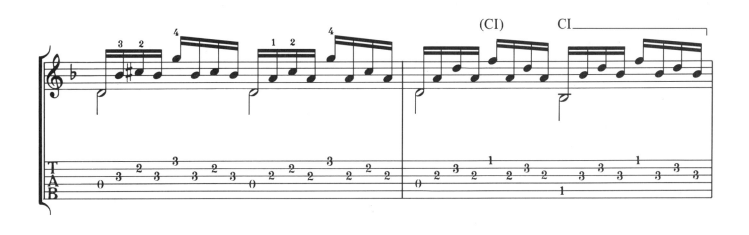

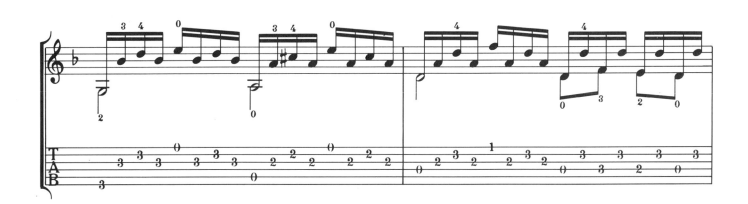

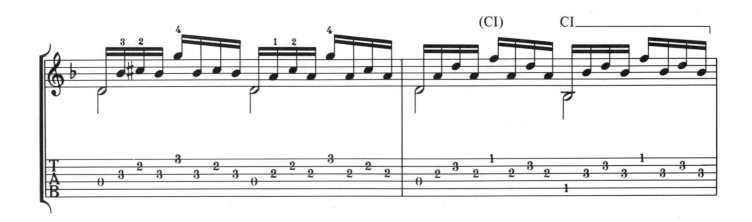

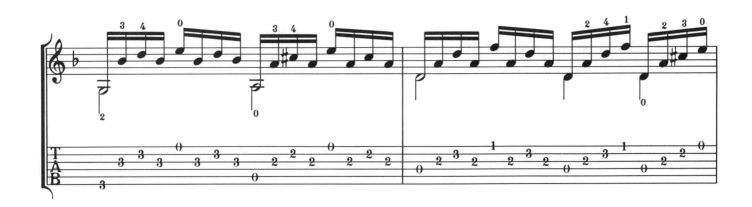

6

STUDY 8

Arr. Ben Bolt

Matteo Carcassi

* Track 6 contains Study 8 and Study 9.

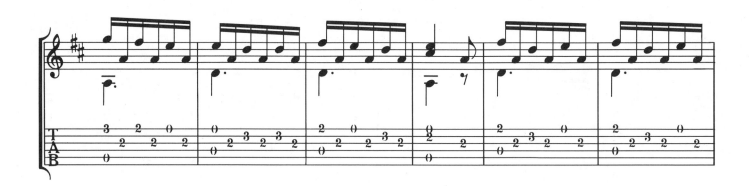

STUDY 9

Arr. Ben Bolt

Mauro Giuliani

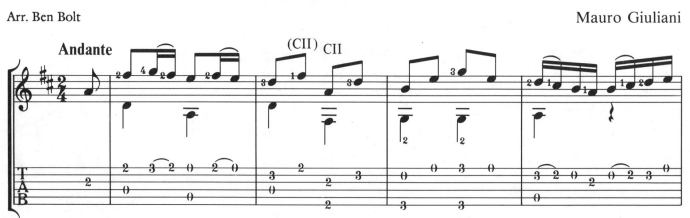

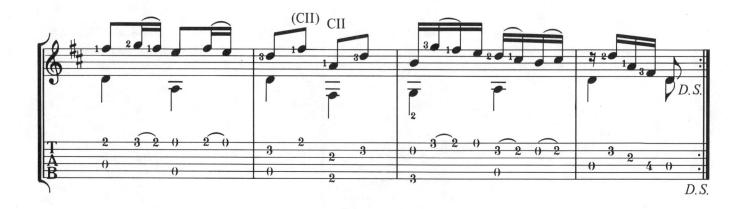

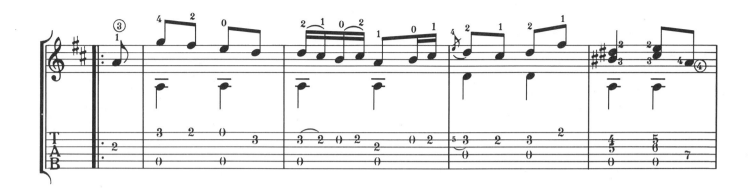

7

STUDY 10

Arr. Ben Bolt

Mauro Giuliani

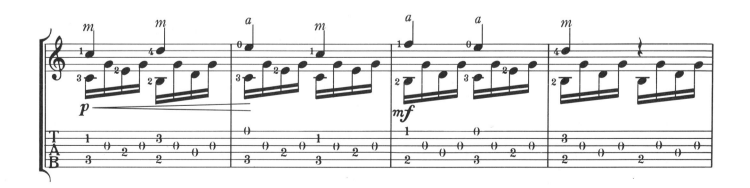

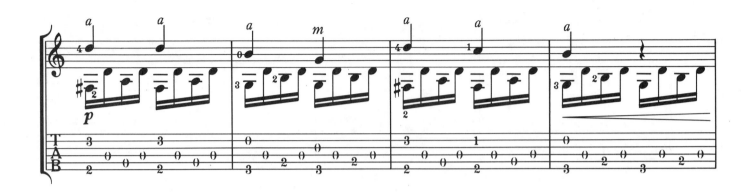

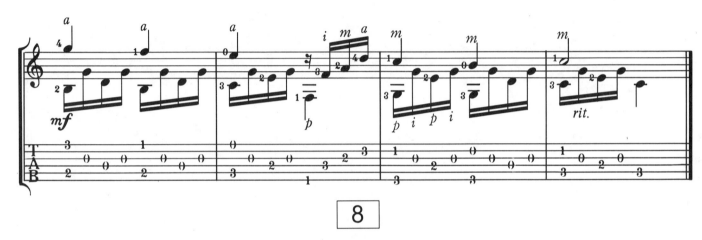

8

STUDY 11

Arr. Ben Bolt

Dionisio Aguado

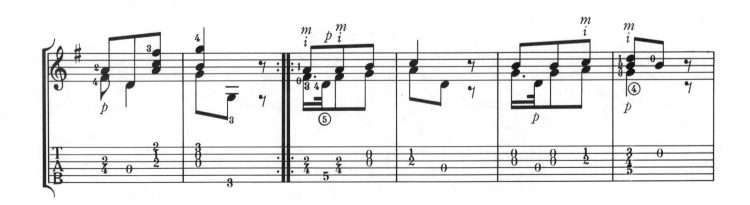

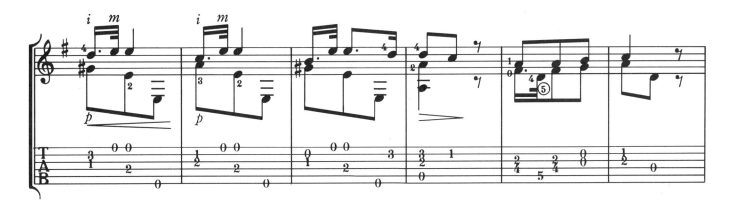

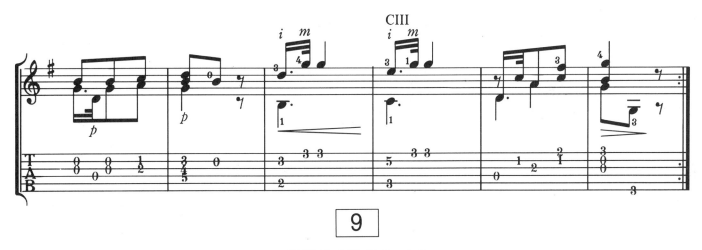

9

STUDY 12

Arr. Ben Bolt

Mauro Giuliani

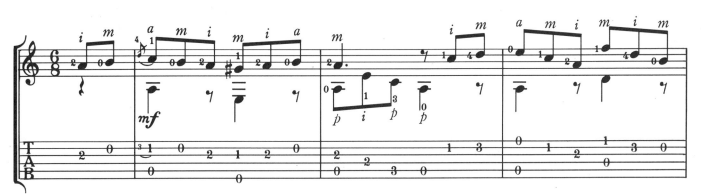

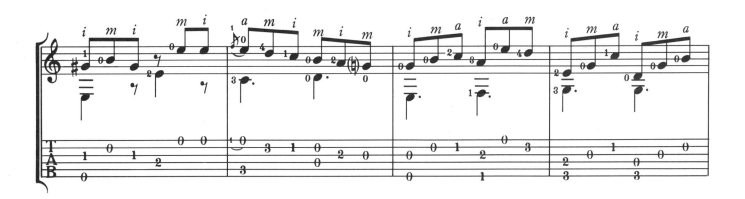

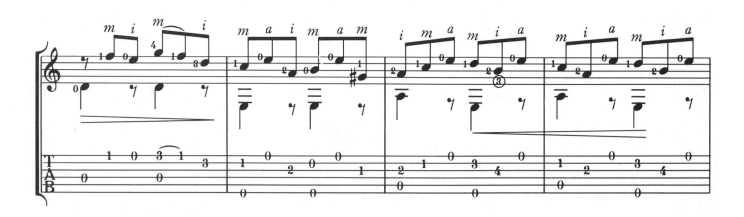

JOYFUL, JOYFUL WE ADORE THEE

Arr. Ben Bolt

Ludwig van Beethoven

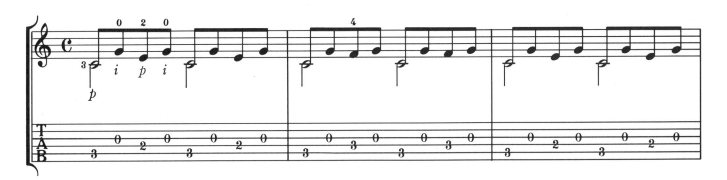

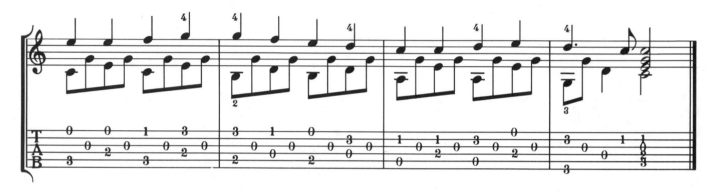

11

RONDO

Arr. Ben Bolt

Matteo Carcassi

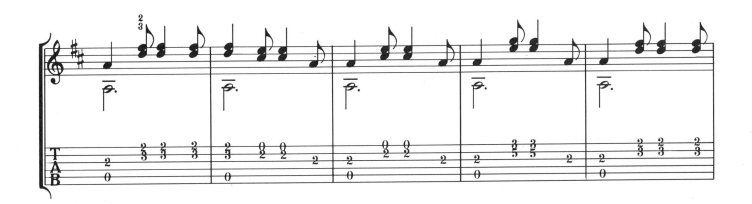

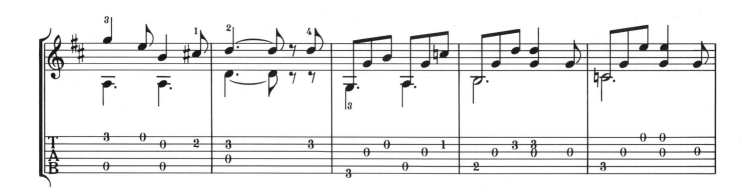

12

ALLEGRETTO

Arr. Ben Bolt

Fernando Carulli

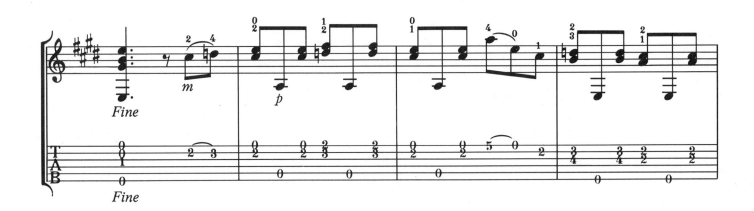

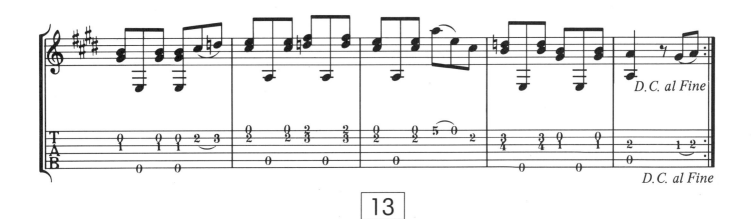

D.C. al Fine

13

WALTZ

Arr. Ben Bolt

Matteo Carcassi

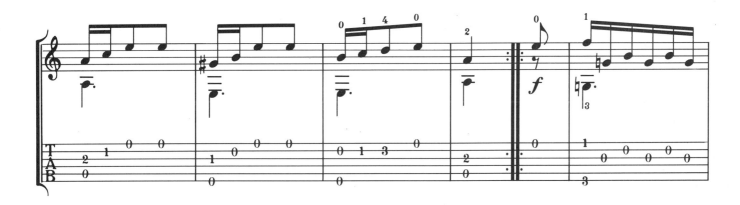

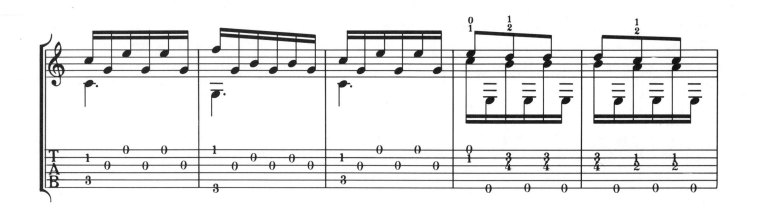

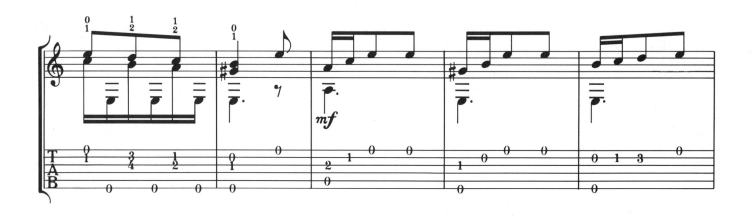

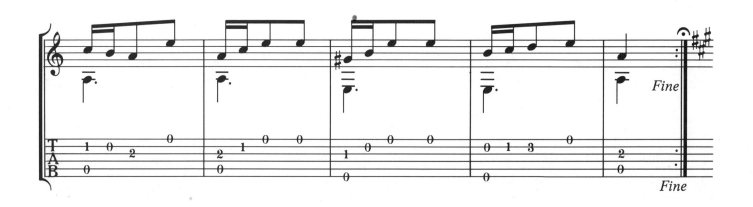

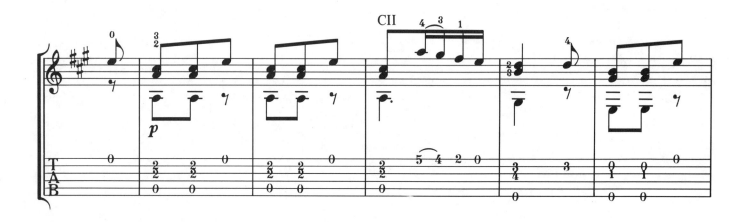

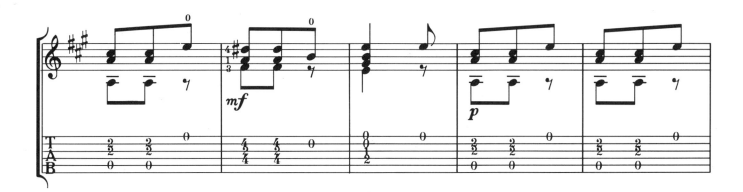

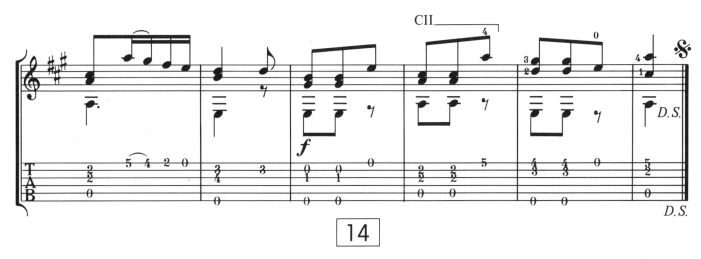

14

MAESTOSO

Arr. Ben Bolt

Mauro Giuliani

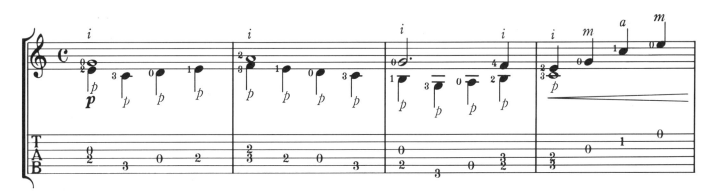

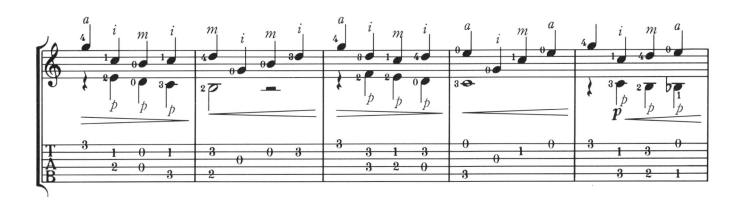

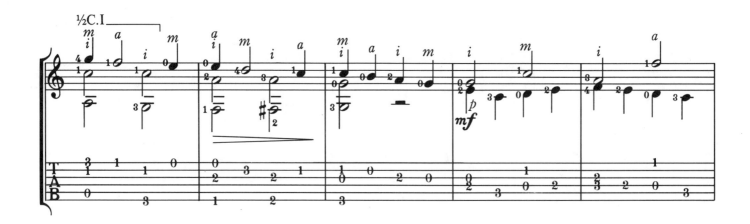

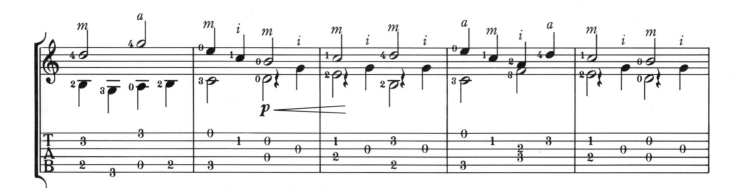

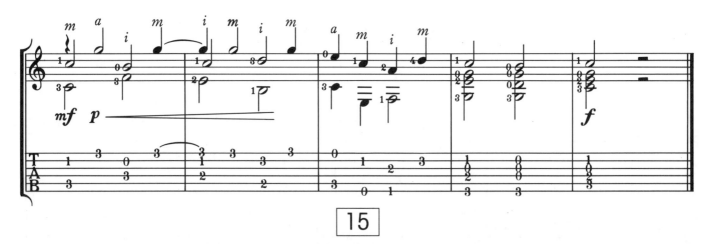

15

SCARBOROUGH FAIR

Arr. Ben Bolt

Anon.

16

VIVACE

Arr. Ben Bolt

Mauro Giuliani

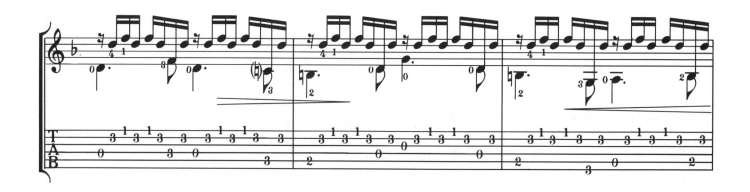

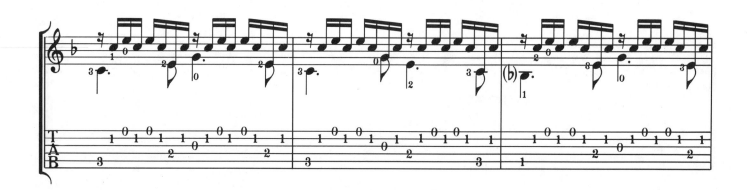

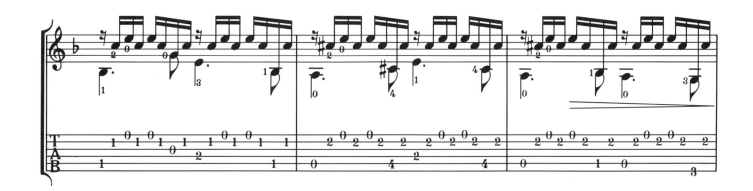

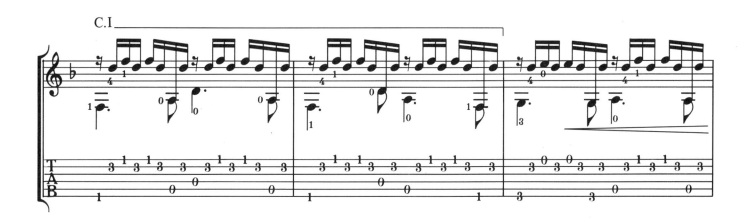

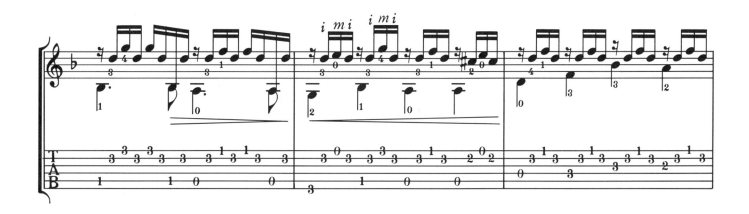

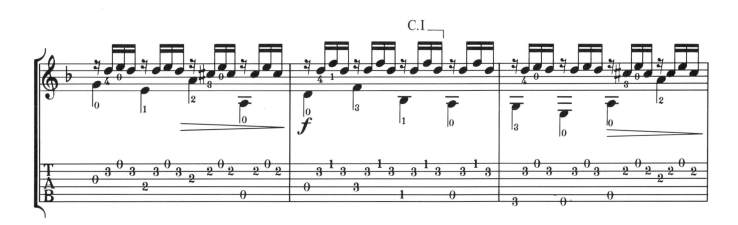

17

ESTUDIO

Arr. Ben Bolt

Fernando Carulli

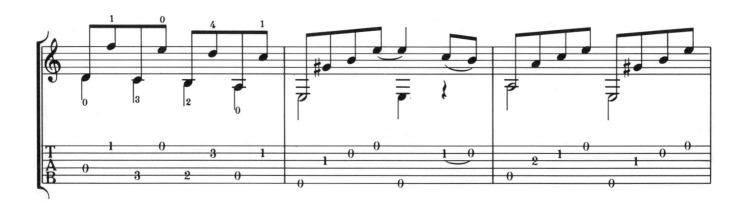

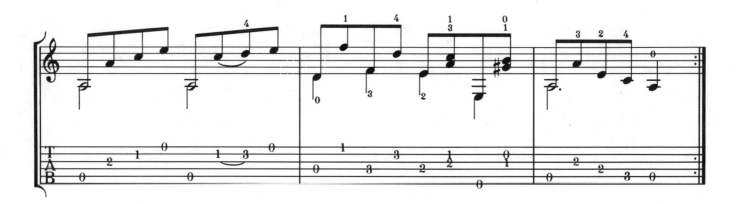

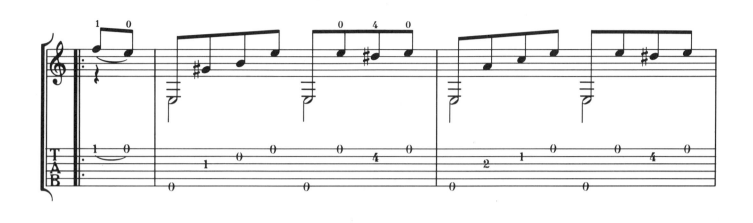

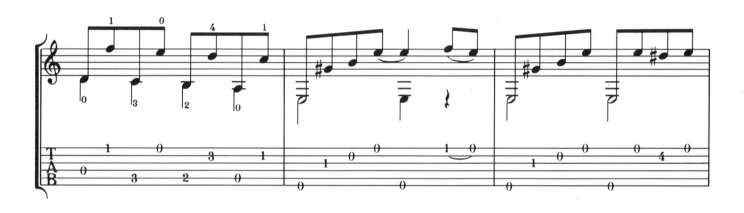

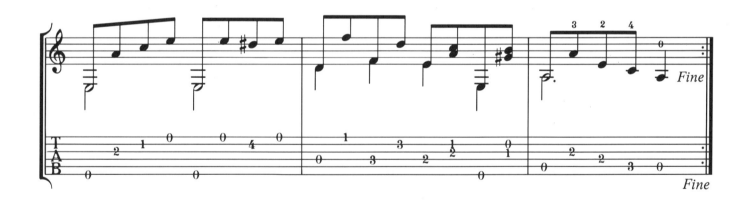

Fine

Fine

D.C. al Fine

18

GRAZIOSO

Arr. Ben Bolt

Mauro Giuliani

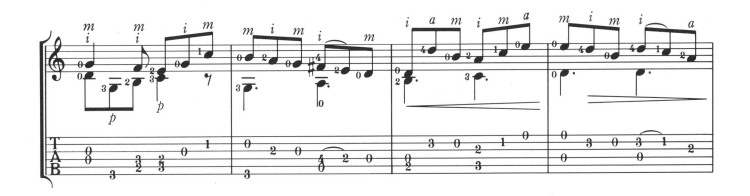

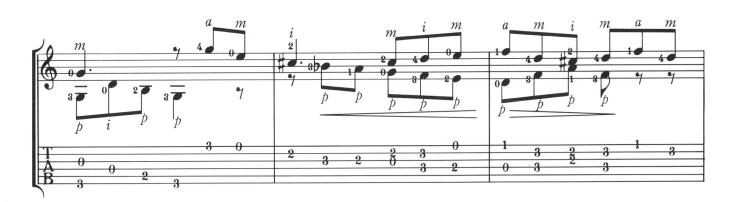

33

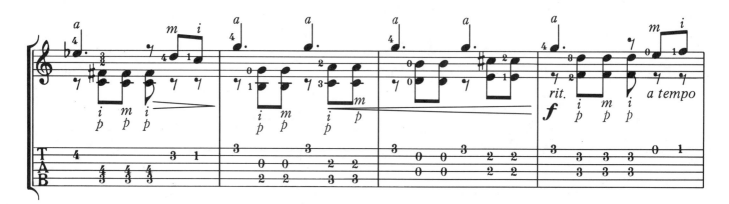

19

ALLEGRO

Arr. Ben Bolt

Mauro Giuliani

$\boxed{20}$

ETUDE

Arr. Ben Bolt

Matteo Carcassi

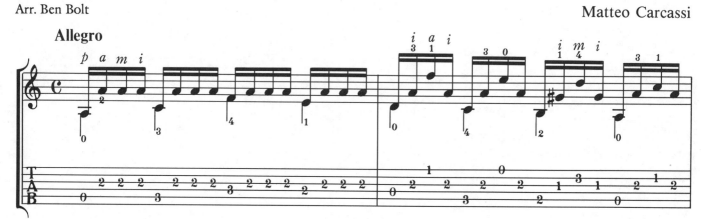

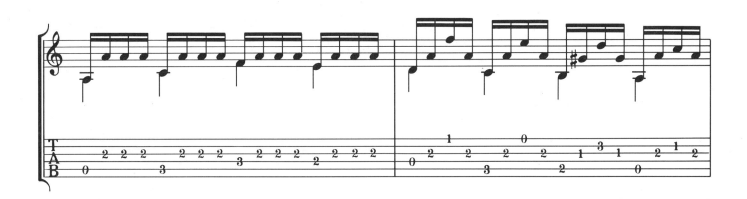

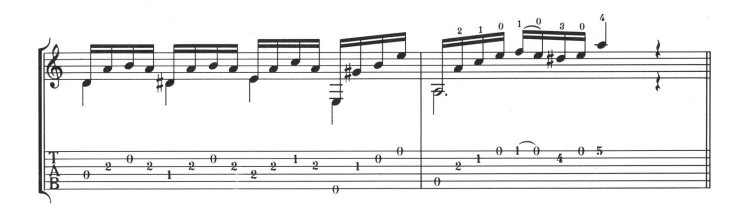

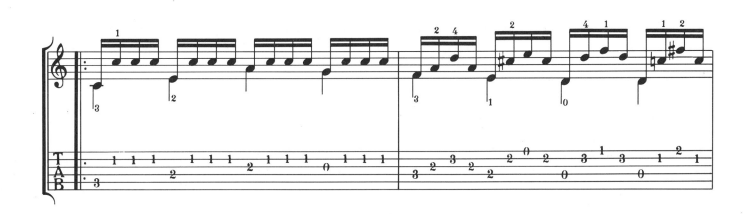

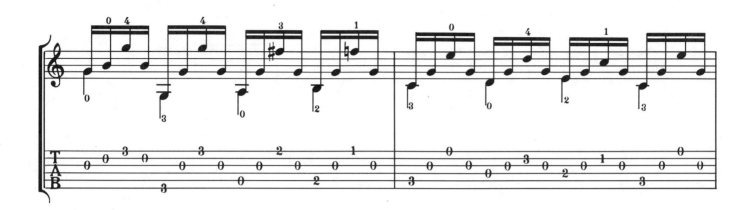

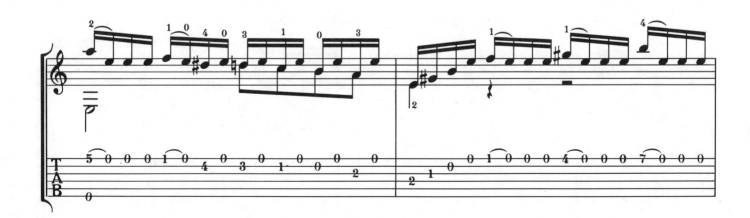

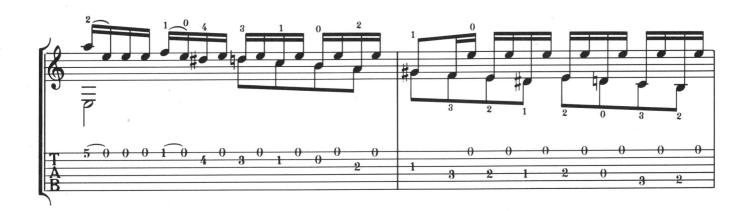

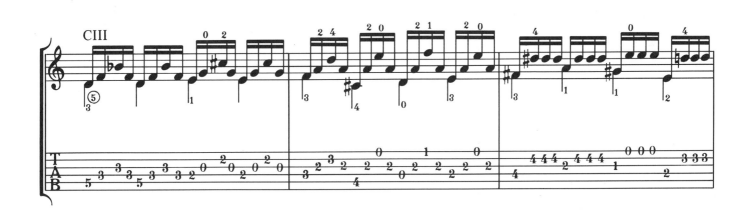

21

LAGRIMA

Francisco Tarrega

Arr. Ben Bolt

Largo

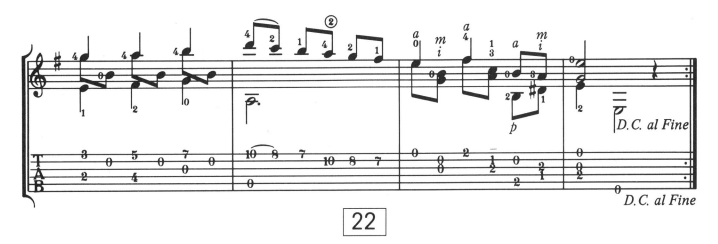

D.C. al Fine

22

MODERATO

Arr. Ben Bolt

Mauro Giuliani

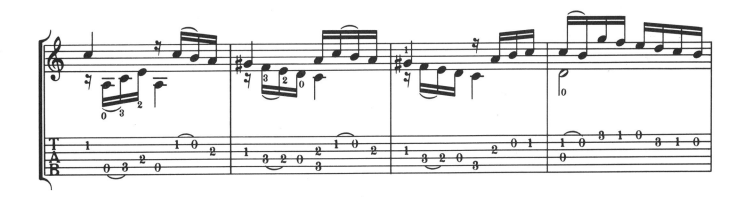

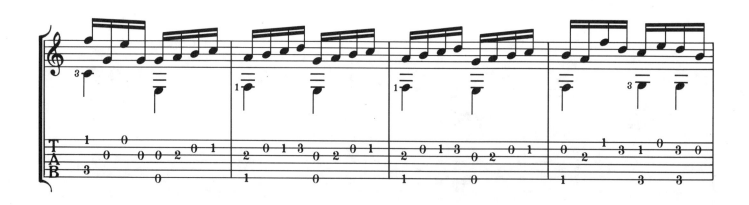

STUDY IN A

Arr. Ben Bolt

Matteo Carcassi

BOUREE

Transcribed by
BEN BOLT (1987)

J. S. Bach

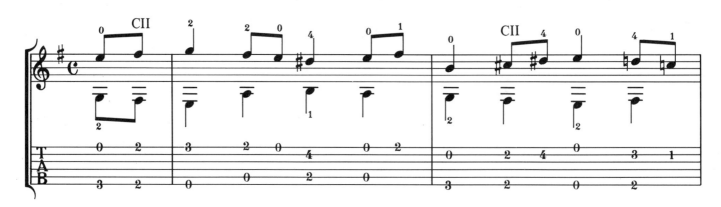

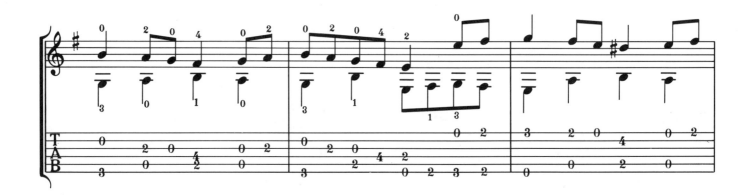

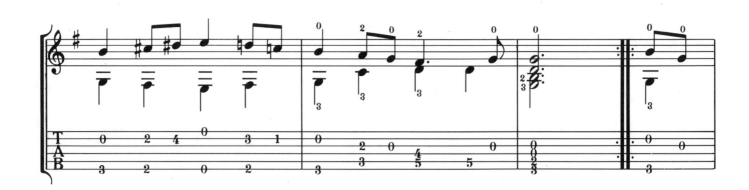

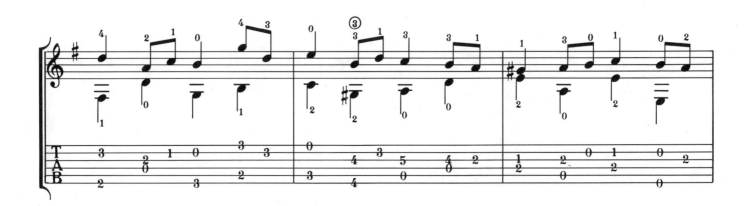

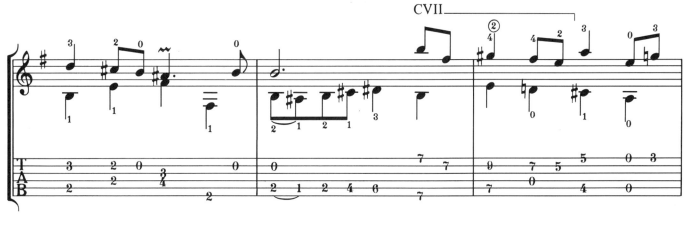

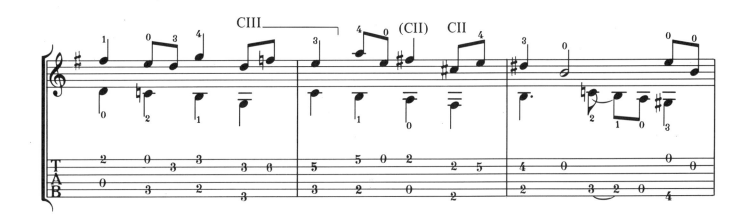

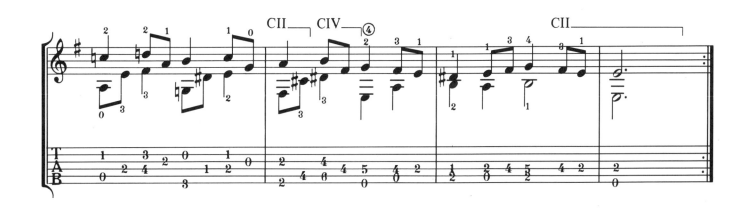

TABLATURE: A six-line staff that graphically represents the guitar fingerboard, with the top line indicating the highest-sounding string (high E). By placing a number on the appropriate line, the string and fret of any note can be indicated. The number 0 represents an open string.

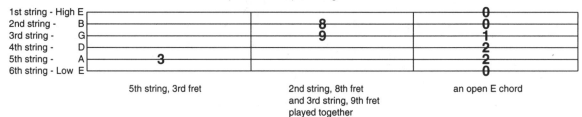

1st string - High E
2nd string - B
3rd string - G
4th string - D
5th string - A
6th string - Low E

5th string, 3rd fret 2nd string, 8th fret an open E chord
       and 3rd string, 9th fret
       played together

Definitions for Special Classical Guitar Notation

Stem Direction and Right-Hand Fingering: In music of two or more parts, notes with downward stems are played by the thumb; notes with upward stems are played by the fingers; a note with a double stem (up and down) is played by the thumb. The letters *p, i, m* and *a* are used to specify which right-hand fingers are to play the indicated notes (*p* = thumb; *i* = index; *m* = middle; *a* = ring).

Barre: The letter *C* and accompanying Roman numeral indicate which fret is to be barred by the left hand. A dotted line indicates how long the barre is to be held.

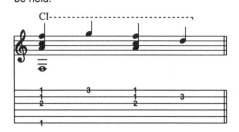

Fractional Barre: The fraction preceding the letter C indicates how many strings the left hand covers when barring. For example, 2/3C means to barre the top four strings, 1/2C the top three strings, etc.

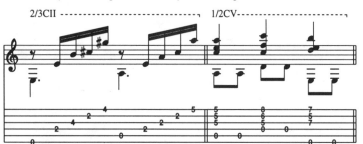

String Numbers and Left-Hand Fingering:
Numbers inside circles indicate on which string a note is to be played, and uncircled numbers indicate which left-hand fingers to use (1 = index; 2 = middle; 3 = ring; 4 = little).

Slurs: An ascending slur is executed by a hammer-on. A descending slur is executed by a pull-off. A straight line connecting two slurred notes indicates a slide.

Arpeggios: A vertical wavy line indicates the notes are to be played quickly by rolling them from bottom to top (no arrowhead present) or top to bottom (arrowhead pointing down).

Harmonic: A harmonic is produced by the left hand lightly touching the string over the node point while simultaneously plucking with the right hand.

Artificial Harmonic: The note is fretted normally and a harmonic is produced by lightly touching the node point with the right-hand index finger while simultaneously plucking with the right-hand middle or ring finger.

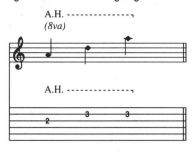

"Ben Bolt is an excellent guitar player, with fine tone."

Andres Segovia

BEN BOLT

Ben Bolt was playing lead guitar in rock bands at age 12 and was performing professionally at age 16 in Miami night clubs.

After graduating from Musica en Compostela, Bolt studied with Abel Carlevaro in Paris. Carlevaro invited him to attend the 1974 International Guitar Seminary in Brazil under full scholarship.

In 1975 Bolt competed with students from 13 countries and won the coveted Merit Prize as Outstanding Student at the First International Masters Class in Montevideo, Uruguay.

Bolt also studied under the direction of Guido Santorsola, the distinguished Italian composer, at the international music conservatory in Montevideo. After graduating with the highest honors, Bolt went on concert tours throughout Central and South America.

At his concert debut in Uruguay, critics proclaimed him to be "a true maestro." A Panama reviewer stated "...he has a rapport with the composer that spells the difference between mere technical ability and virtuosity."

Bolt is an endorsee of Takamine guitars, Trace acoustic amps, and D'Addario strings. He records for Rosemary Records. His books and tapes are distributed worldwide through major music publishers.

Bolt resides in Knoxville, Tennessee, where he teaches all styles of guitar. He is also Professor of Guitar at Carson-Newman College in Jefferson City, Tennessee.

$17.95 in U.S.
Book and CD
ISBN 0-89524-741-0

0 73999 06915 0

02506915
Printed in the U.S.

Cherry Lane Music Company
• *Quality In Printed Music* •
P.O. Box 430, Port Chester, NY 10573

EXCLUSIVELY DISTRIBUTED BY

HAL•LEONARD CORPORATION
7777 W. BLUEMOUND RD. P.O. BOX 13819 MILWAUKEE, WI 53213